Biggest, Baddest Books for Boys

BIGGEST, BADDEST BOOK OF

BUGS

ANDERS HANSON & ELISSA MANN

Consulting Editor, Diane Craig, M.A./Reading Specialist

A Division of ABDO

ABDO
Publishing Company

visit us at www.abdopublishing.com

Published by ABDO Publishing Company, a division of ABDO, P.O. Box 398166,
Minneapolis, Minnesota 55439. Copyright © 2013 by Abdo Consulting Group, Inc.
International copyrights reserved in all countries. No part of this book may be
reproduced in any form without written permission from the publisher. Super
SandCastle™ is a trademark and logo of ABDO Publishing Company.

Printed in the United States of America, North Mankato, Minnesota
062012
092012

Editor: Liz Salzmann
Content Developer: Nancy Tuminelly
Cover and Interior Design and Production: Anders Hanson, Mighty Media, Inc.
Illustration Credits: Shutterstock

Library of Congress Cataloging-in-Publication Data
Hanson, Anders, 1980-
  Biggest, baddest book of bugs / Anders Hanson and Elissa Mann.
     p. cm. -- (Biggest, baddest books for boys)
  ISBN 978-1-61783-405-9 (alk. paper)
  1. Insects--Juvenile literature. I. Mann, Elissa, 1990- II. Title. III. Series: Biggest,
baddest books.
  QL467.2.H36 2012
  595.7--dc23
                    2011050903

Super SandCastle™ books are created by a team of professional educators, reading specialists, and
content developers around five essential components—phonemic awareness, phonics, vocabulary, text
comprehension, and fluency—to assist young readers as they develop reading skills and strategies and
increase their general knowledge. All books are written, reviewed, and leveled for guided reading, early reading
intervention, and Accelerated Reader® programs for use in shared, guided, and independent reading and
writing activities to support a balanced approach to literacy instruction.

CONTENTS

BUGS!

Bugs are creepy **critters**. They can be found all over Earth. Even in your home or backyard. Some are gross or scary. Some are beautiful. But they are all **amazing**!

Caterpillar

Trap door spider

A bug has an exoskeleton. That means its skeleton is on the outside of its body. The exoskeleton is tough. It protects and supports the bug's body.

Scarab beetle

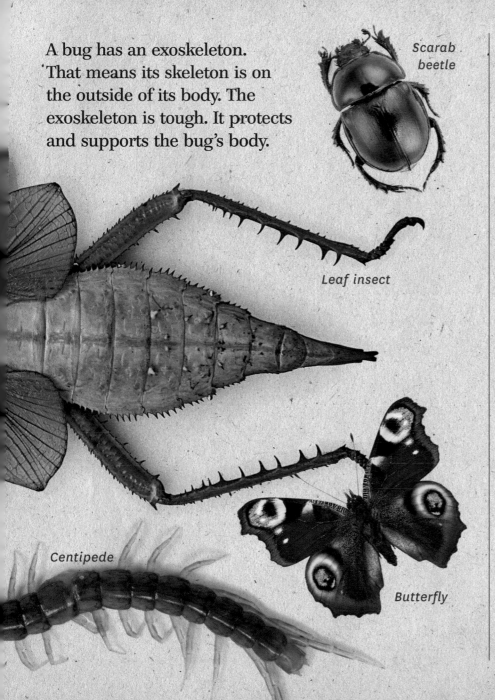

Leaf insect

Centipede

Butterfly

WHAT'S A BUG?

Bugs include insects, arachnids, and myriapods.

INSECTS

- six legs
- may or may not have wings
- antennae
- three body **segment**s

ARACHNIDS

- eight legs
- no wings
- no antennae
- two body segments

MYRIAPODS

- many legs
- no wings
- antennae
- many body segments

Bugs Abound

Bugs come in all colors, shapes, and sizes! For every person, there are more than 200 million bugs!

Bug Collection

Many people collect bugs. They like to study the bugs up close.

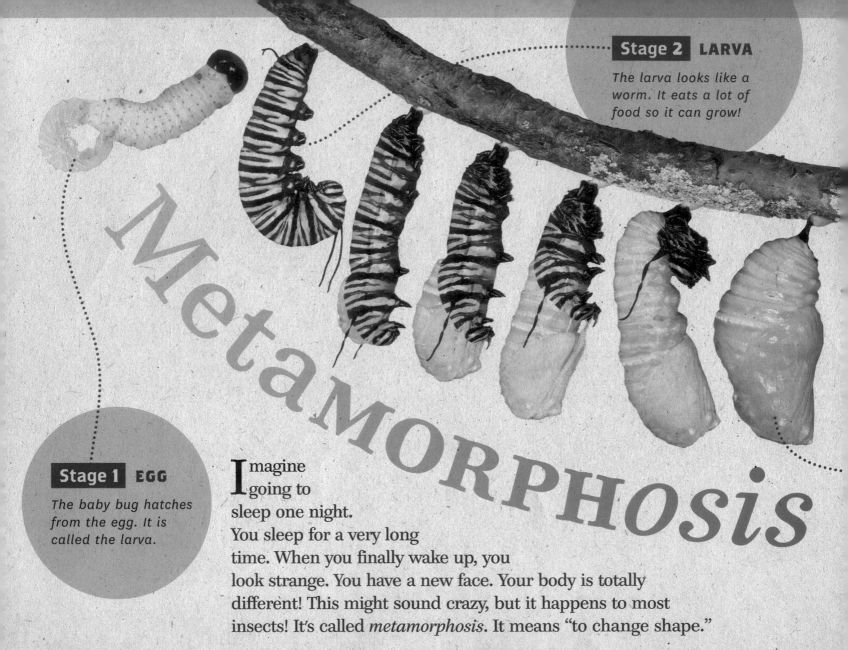

Stage 2 LARVA

The larva looks like a
worm. It eats a lot of
food so it can grow!

MetaMORPHOSiS

Stage 1 EGG

The baby bug hatches
from the egg. It is
called the larva.

Imagine going to sleep one night. You sleep for a very long time. When you finally wake up, you look strange. You have a new face. Your body is totally different! This might sound crazy, but it happens to most insects! It's called *metamorphosis*. It means "to change shape."

Many insects go through four stages of metamorphosis. This is what a monarch butterfly's metamorphosis looks like.

Stage 3 PUPA

The pupa sheds its exoskeleton. The exoskeleton makes a case called a chrysalis. The bug rests inside while it changes.

Stage 4 IMAGO

Over time, the chrysalis becomes clear. Then the bug comes out. It is fully grown!

Walking stick

Geometer moth

Leaf mimic katydid

CAMOUFLAGE

Wolf spider

Leaf insect

Malaysian jungle nymph

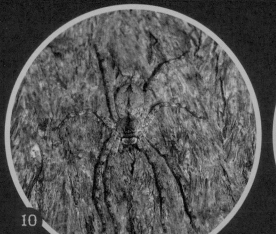

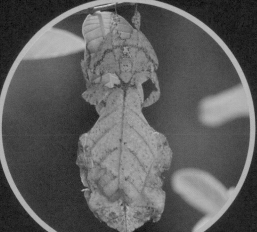

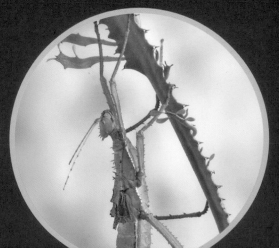

Hawk moth

Lappet

Brimstone butterfly

ome bugs match their surroundings. It's called *camouflage*. Camouflage helps bugs hide from predators.

Can you see the bugs on these pages? They may look like sticks, leaves, bark, or rocks. There's one in every picture!

Slant-faced grasshopper

White-clouded longhorn beetle

Orchid mantis

STICK INSECTS

Stick insects look like plants! It is hard for predators to see them.

Some stick insects can grow new legs. This helps them get away if a predator grabs them. They just leave a leg or two behind!

GIANT PRICKLY STICK INSECT

The giant prickly stick insect can grow up to 8 inches (20 cm) long. Many people keep them as pets!

GIANT PRICKLY
STICK INSECT

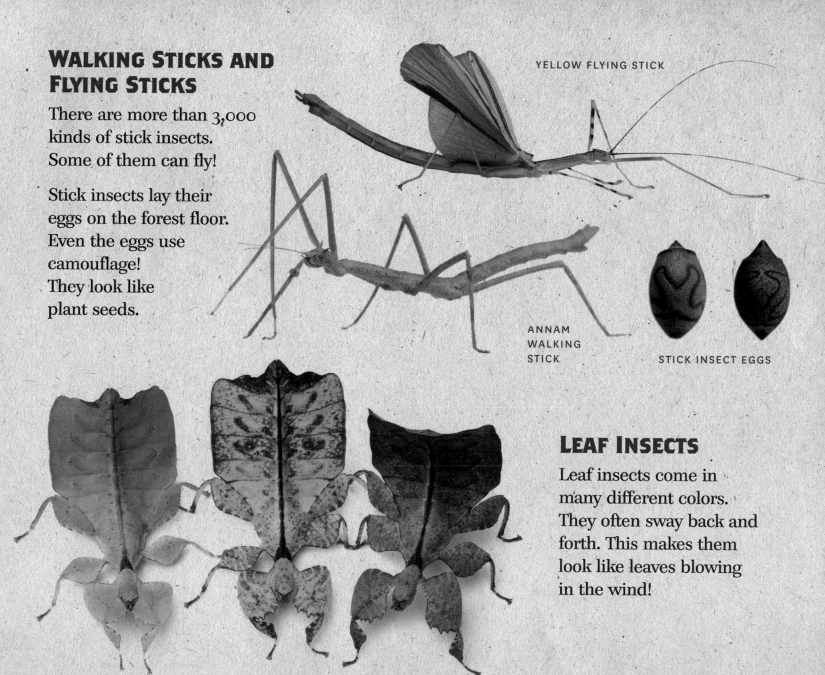

WALKING STICKS AND FLYING STICKS

There are more than 3,000 kinds of stick insects. Some of them can fly!

Stick insects lay their eggs on the forest floor. Even the eggs use camouflage! They look like plant seeds.

YELLOW FLYING STICK

ANNAM WALKING STICK

STICK INSECT EGGS

LEAF INSECTS

Leaf insects come in many different colors. They often sway back and forth. This makes them look like leaves blowing in the wind!

13

Glow in the Dark

Some bugs are bioluminescent. This means that they can make their own light. In the dark, these bugs glow!

FIREFLIES

Fireflies light up to **attract** other fireflies.
Fireflies are not actually flies, they are beetles.
They are also called lightning bugs.

MILLIPEDES

Millipedes have between 36 and 400 legs! Some millipedes glow in the dark. The glow warns other animals to stay away.

CLICK BEETLES

Certain click beetles have two glowing spots. They can change how brightly the spots glow.

SCORPIONS

Scorpions aren't bioluminescent. But they can still glow in the dark! They are fluorescent. They only glow under ultraviolet light. People use ultraviolet lamps to find scorpions in the dark.

BUG EYES!

DRAGONFLY

HOUSE FLY

ALL EYES ON YOU!

Insects have compound eyes. This means that many little lenses make up each eye. A human eye has only one lens.

WHAT BIG EYES YOU HAVE!

A dragonfly's eyes take up most of its head. Each eye has thousands of little lenses. Each lens sees a different angle. A dragonfly can look in many directions at once.

LITTLE EYES TOO!

Many bugs have simple eyes too. A simple eye only has one lens.

HORNET

STALK-EYED FLY

EYE ON A STICK

The stalk-eyed fly has two stalks on its head. Each stalk has an eye at the end of it!

BEE BALLET

Can you tell your friends where to find food with a dance? Bees can! When a bee finds food, it dances around.

The other bees watch the dance. They aren't trying to learn its moves. They want to know where they can find food!

The round dance tells other bees that food is close by.

The waggle dance shows that food is far away. The longer the dance, the farther from the hive the food is!

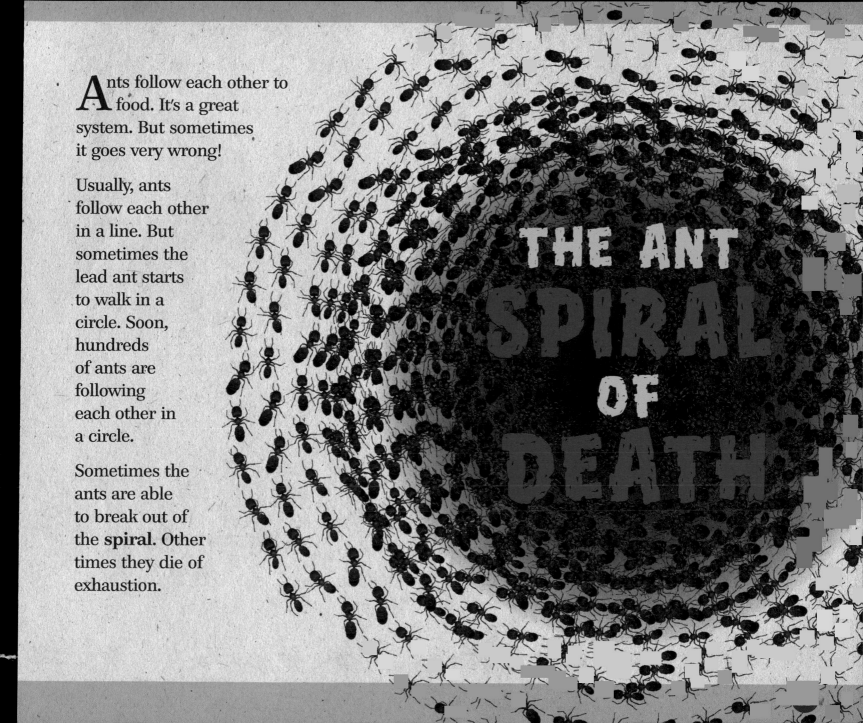

Ants follow each other to food. It's a great system. But sometimes it goes very wrong!

Usually, ants follow each other in a line. But sometimes the lead ant starts to walk in a circle. Soon, hundreds of ants are following each other in a circle.

Sometimes the ants are able to break out of the **spiral**. Other times they die of exhaustion.

THE ANT SPIRAL OF DEATH

FARMER ANT

An ant brings a leaf back to its colony. Another ant tears it into tiny pieces.

LEAFCUTTER ANT

The leafcutter ant grows its own food! It is the only non-human creature that farms.

Leafcutter ant colonies can have up to 15 million ants! Each ant has a special job to do in the colony.

Then the ant puts the pieces in a special **chamber**. This is the **fungus** garden.

As the leaf rots, the fungus grows! The ants use some of the fungus for food.

The ants bring their trash to dump chambers.

BUG BUFFET!

GRASSHOPPERS

Many people in Asia and Africa think grasshoppers taste great! The bugs are fried and sprayed with a sauce.

BAMBOO WORMS

Bamboo worms are not really worms. They are moth pupae. They live in bamboo shoots. They are eaten by many people in Thailand.

SILKWORMS

Silkworms are also moth pupae. They are a **delicacy** in many Asian countries.

BUGS UP CLOSE

Check out these crazy bug faces! See if you can guess what kinds of bugs they belong to. It's not easy. Look below for the answers.

A

B

C

D

E

F

WHAT DO YOU KNOW ABOUT BUGS?

1. INSECTS HAVE EIGHT LEGS. **TRUE OR FALSE?**

2. A COMPOUND EYE HAS ONE LENS. **TRUE OR FALSE?**

3. SCORPIONS ARE FLUORESCENT. **TRUE OR FALSE?**

4. MANY PEOPLE EAT GRASSHOPPERS. **TRUE OR FALSE?**

ANSWERS: 1) FALSE 2) FALSE 3) TRUE 4) TRUE

GLOSSARY

AMAZING – wonderful or surprising.

ATTRACT – to cause someone or something to come near.

CHAMBER – an enclosed space or section.

CRITTER – any animal.

DELICACY – a food that is a rare or special treat to eat.

FUNGUS – an organism, such as mold or mildew, that grows on rotting plants.

SEGMENT – a section or part of something.

SPIRAL – a pattern that winds in a circle.

LEOPARDS

LEOPARDS

MARY ANN McDONALD

THE CHILD'S WORLD®

A herd of deerlike impala drink at an African waterhole. One impala suddenly jerks up its head. The impala snorts a warning call. The herd comes to attention. Within seconds, the herd runs away. What scared the impala? A leopard quietly walks out of a nearby bush.

Leopards live in more areas of the world than any other big cat. Leopards are found in many parts of Africa, southern Asia, China, and Korea. They live in rainforests, jungles, mountains, grasslands, and even cities and towns. Leopards roam from sea level to the highest mountains.

Leopards are shy animals. They are mostly *nocturnal,* or active at night. Leopards like to hide in trees or bushes during the day. Many people never see a leopard when they go to Africa.

Leopards are tan and have many dark spots. The spots help a leopard hide. Some leopards that live in thick jungles are black. The spots on a black leopard are hard to see.

Leopards are *predators*, which means that they hunt other animals. Leopards hunt by sneaking up on, or *stalking*, an animal very quietly. Leopards can't run very fast for very long. They must be very close to an animal to catch it. Sometimes a leopard waits patiently for something to walk by.

A leopard attacks by leaping from a hiding place and knocking the animal down with its front legs. The leopard grabs the animal's throat and bites down hard. The animal can't breathe and soon dies.

Leopards are *carnivores*, or meat eaters. They eat insects, reptiles, birds, monkeys, small mammals, and larger grass-eating animals. Leopards that live in cities eat dogs and stray cats. Sometimes, leopards become man-eaters. This only happens when there is no other food for the leopards to eat.

Leopards are the weight-lifters of the cat world. An average leopard weighs around 100 pounds. It can kill an animal that weighs almost 300 pounds! Some leopards carry their food up into trees. Leopards must be very strong to do this. Could you wrestle your father and win? Could you then drag him up a tree?

A leopard hangs its food in a tree so other animals won't eat it. The leopard grabs the neck of the dead animal in its mouth. Using its claws and powerful front legs, the leopard climbs the tree head-first, carrying the kill. This food will feed the leopard for several days.

Leopards have many enemies. Baboons, lions, and hyenas will attack baby leopards. These animals will also kill an adult leopard if they get the chance. Pythons also eat leopards. People, though, are the leopard's greatest enemies. Leopards almost became extinct when people hunted them for their beautiful spotted coats. Laws have now stopped the hunting and saved the big cats.

Leopards are *solitary*, living alone for most of their lives. Leopards live in territories. A *territory* is a special area that a leopard calls home. A male and a female come together only to mate. Three months later, the female gives birth to one to three cubs. The cubs are born blind, deaf, and unable to walk.

A mother leopard hides her cubs for the first six weeks. She uses caves, hollow trees, or dense bushes to hide them. The mother leopard leaves them for several hours each day while she hunts. It is a scary time for the cubs! The cubs drink their mother's milk when they are small. After three months, they start eating meat.

The young cubs play and learn to climb trees. They follow their mother and learn to hunt. The mother leopard walks with her tail curled up and held high. Her cubs see the white tail and follow her. Even in tall grass, the cubs don't get lost.

Leopard cubs stay with their mother for nearly two years. Even after they leave, the mother helps them find food for the next several months.

Leopards communicate in many ways. They mark their territories by spraying urine on bushes. Other cats smell this and know who lives in the area. Leopards also use their bodies to communicate. They twitch their tails, arch their backs, or lay back their ears. Other cats understand these signals and stay away.

Leopards make many sounds. They grunt, growl, snarl, and hiss. Young cubs may meow for their mother. Leopards also make a special sound when they want to be heard far away. This call is a rasping cough that sounds like someone sawing wood.

The *clouded leopard* and the *snow leopard* are close cousins to the leopard. The clouded leopard, like the one shown here, lives in southeast Asia's rainforests. It climbs trees to hunt birds and monkeys. The snow leopard lives in the Himalayan Mountains of Asia, wherever there is a lot of snow. It eats marmots and mountain sheep.

Many of the world's wild cats are in trouble. Some are still hunted for their beautiful coats. Others are losing their habitats to people. Luckily, the leopard has hope. It can live in many different places and eat many different things. With our help, the leopard will survive. Then we can all enjoy one of the world's most beautiful wild cats, the leopard.

INDEX

Photographs by Joe McDonald

Text Copyright © 1996 by The Child's World®, Inc.
All rights reserved. No part of this book may be reproduced
or utilized in any form or by any means without written
permission from the publisher.
Printed in the United States of America.

Library of Congress Cataloging-in-Publication Data
Available upon Request.

ISBN 1-56766-211-0